UNDER HIS SHADOW

WRITINGS

Volume 1

by David Mayorga

Published by

SHABAR PUBLICATIONS

www.shabarpublications.com

Most Shabar Publications products are available at special quantity discounts for bulk purchase for sales promotions, fund-raising and educational needs. For details, write Shabar Publications at mayorga1126@gmail.com.

Under His Shadow Writings Series Volume 1 *by David Mayorga*
Published by Shabar Publications
3833 N. Taylor Rd.
Palmhurst, Texas 78573
www.shabarpublications.com
www.masterbuildertx.com

Edited by Emily Rose King

ISBN 978-1-7333174-9-8

Table of Contents

Introduction 5
Day 1: Am I One of God's Ringleaders? 8
Day 2: What Is Holding Me Back? 11
Day 3: Stepping into Him! 14
Day 4: The Spirit of Willingness! 17
Day 5: The Power of Forgiveness! 20
Day 6: Keep Praying Until 23
Day 7: Times to Stand Still and Consider! 26
Day 8: We Are in His Hands! 29
Day 9: The Violent Fire of His Presence 32
Day 10: What a Finish! 35
Day 11: An Unquenchable Fire! 38
Day 12: In All Things, Give Thanks! 41
Day 13: God's Mending Business! 44
Day 14: Experiencing More of Him! 47
Day 15: Living Inside God's Sphere & Timing! 50
Day 16: From the Dust of the Ground 53
Day 17: Recognizing the Wiles of the Devil 56
Day 18: The Call to Faithfulness! 59
Day 19: Always Before Me! 62
Day 20: Until I'm Satisfied! 65

Day 21: It's About His Power! ... 68
Day 22: I Will Wait! ... 71
Day 23: I Love Him, but Do I Respect Him? ... 74
Day 24: One Thing I Desire! ... 77
Day 25: The Art of Twisting! ... 80
Day 26: The Vision of the Rock ... 83
Day 27: Precious Things Have an Expensive Price! ... 86
Day 28: In the Likeness of His Resurrection! ... 89
Day 29: Overcoming Disappointments! ... 92
Day 30: The Excellency of the Knowledge of Christ! ... 95
Day 31: Overcoming the Spirit of Lawlessness! ... 98
Day 32: The Meek! ... 101
Day 33: What an Amazing Love! ... 104
Day 34: Lord, Open My Eyes! ... 107
Day 35: Led by the Spirit! ... 110
Day 36: Don't Get Tired! ... 113
Day 37: The Overcomer! ... 116
Day 38: God Is for Me! ... 119
Day 39: Never Neglect the Spiritual Man! ... 122
Day 40: Learning to Lean! ... 126
Ministry Resources ... 130
Ministry Information ... 131

Introduction

"As the apple tree among the trees of the wood,
So is my beloved among the sons.
I sat down under his shadow with great delight,
And his fruit was sweet to my taste."
(Song of Solomon 2:3)

In spending forty days and forty nights in prayer and fasting, I felt led by the Spirit to journal my encounters with God during this season of consecration. All my notes came out of spending time in prayer and finding intimate moments in His presence. The dreams and visions came from this season of seeking God as well. Hunger for more of Jesus led me to do this fast, nothing else. May His kingdom be advanced because of this insignificant effort!

As my heart yearns after God, I wonder . . .

Is there anything better on this side of heaven, than for a man or woman of God to occupy themselves in the knowledge of Christ, the Lord? Is there anything more valuable in this life or more worth our time, than investing our hearts in getting to know God more intimately? I think not!

Many might not agree with my statement or my opinion in regards to knowing God more intimately, but trust me, after walking hand in hand with the Lord for over thirty-five years, I have discovered that much of our desires, ambitions, and goals, are nothing more than flesh! As pure and as noble we might think our plans are, there is something selfish lurking behind it all.

In the world system we live in, the more you have, the better. The more you accomplish in the sight of man, the higher your status will be. It's a world where the strong demolish the weak without any regrets.

This worldly kingdom has only one thing in mind to exalt the individual-self and increase in outward works for its own glory. The kingdom of God works with a different philosophy, as John the Baptist outlined it: **"He must increase, but I must decrease."** (John 3:30)

We all know that salvation is free, but intimacy with God will not be found on the For Sale table. Intimacy with God entails a life of seeking hard after God. Unless one is willing to die to self, they will not know God in deeper ways!

Now to keep this philosophy alive in the heart of the believer—a life of fasting, prayer, rich times meditating in God's Word, and being quick to obey all that God says— this is the only remedy to advancing His kingdom on earth!

You see, unless a man is willing to forsake himself, his status, his good name, and his place in history, he will struggle to be intimate with God. It is a challenge to be a servant to two masters. You already know the story: You will love one and hate the other, or you will love the other and hate the one. Remember, God will not be intimate with unfaithful lovers!

If we make it our aim to know the Lord in a more intimate way, His fire will purify our hearts. It will consume our thoughts, our emotions, and our desires! Get to know the Lord!

David Mayorga, Author & Teacher
McAllen, Texas

Day 1

Am I One of God's Ringleaders?

"For we have found this man [the Apostle Paul] a plague, a creator of dissension among all the Jews throughout the world, and a ringleader of the sect of the Nazarenes." (Acts 24:5)

On this first day of meeting the Lord for a season of fasting, prayer and intercession, I came across this portion of Scripture regarding the Apostle Paul and the many haters who were unleashing threats against him for preaching Christ without apologies!

I believe it to be an inevitable thing to receive such backlash from the enemy, when the gates of hell are in danger of losing territory. When advancement is made for the kingdom of God, the enemy will reveal its ugly head against God's servant and malign, criticize, and make every attempt to destroy them. In this case, it was the Apostle Paul, the ringleader! Believe me, the devil knows who the real ringleaders for

God are!

The opposite is true of a man who is full of religion but with no fire! He sits pretty without any attacks whatsoever, and goes on with his life and ministry without a care in the world. Why is this? Why is it that some men are attacked more severely than others?

I believe that the man who has been marked by God will also be marked by Satan, thus making him a target for the rest of his days on earth. If you, as a man of God, make the effort to advance God's work, and all hell will come after you. Decide now whom you will serve: Will you serve yourself, or will you serve Jesus, the Lord?

Walk It Out!

Today my goal is to renew my vows to King Jesus. My vow is that today I make Him not only Savior, but Lord of all in my life. I yield my rights to Him! All my dreams, my ambitions, my plans, my desires, and everything He has entrusted me with thus far. All are His, and He can continue to build them or destroy them as He sees fit.

My Prayer

Make me one of God's ringleaders in my generation. Holy Spirit, I'm begging you to release the fire of Your glory upon my head, until I have declared your power to the next generation! I don't want to leave this earth without making an impact for you! Amen.

Day 2

What Is Holding Me Back?

"Then he said to me, 'Do not fear, Daniel, for from the first day that you set your heart to understand, and to humble yourself before your God, your words were heard; and I have come because of your words. But the prince of the kingdom of Persia withstood me twenty-one days; and behold, Michael, one of the chief princes, came to help me, for I had been left alone there with the kings of Persia. Now I have come to make you understand what will happen to your people in the latter days, for the vision refers to many days yet to come.'" (Daniel 10:12-14)

Have you ever felt like you needed to get to a certain place, but for some reason or another, you never got there? You did this over and over again until suddenly you realized that something was blocking you from getting there, something invisible, if you will?

In my hour of prayer this morning, I had this realization

while I stood before the Lord. I have had a desire in my heart to meet God, to become more intimate with Him, but as of late, I have felt that there is something supernatural blocking me from getting there.

I first checked my heart to make sure that there was no sin in my life; I covered myself in the blood of Jesus. As far as I am concerned, there is nothing off between my heavenly Father and me.

It was here where I discerned and recognized that there is a spiritual force (principality or power) preventing me from getting to the place where my heart longs and yearns to be!

I remembered Daniel in his own experience, back when he needed understanding for the deeper things of God— he humbled himself and prayed. The prayer was heard, but the answer was blocked from getting to Daniel for twenty-one days. Who did this? The Bible called it the Prince of Persia— a principality, a spiritual force.

It was not until Michael, the chief prince, came to help, that the answer was released, and then the revelation came forth. Definitely something to consider in your secret time with God.

Walk It Out!

Is there a need to evaluate your spiritual condition before the Lord? Is there a feeling that something is hindering your progress? Your desire to see God's will played-out in your life may be intact, but your forward progress is not happening. Have you considered that perhaps a principality or power may also be hindering your life as it happened to Daniel? Search your heart as you seek God for this unveiling.

My Prayer

King Jesus, this morning I come before Your glorious throne to humble myself before you. Will you allow me to see and discern the spiritual realm around me? — I sense that there is a hindrance or an obstacle in my progress in getting to know You. Whatever is hidden in the spiritual realm, help me to see it so that I may tear it down in Your name, Jesus! Amen.

Day 3

Stepping into Him!

"Abide in Me, and I in you. As the branch cannot bear fruit of itself, unless it abides in the vine, neither can you, unless you abide in Me." (John 15:4)

This morning during my quiet time with God, I felt the strong empowering words of Jesus speak loudly to my heart. As I worshiped and adored Him, the Lord made me realize how this one truth must be the first order of the day for any true follower of His!

It is one thing for us to abide in Him and call Him Savior and Lord and to praise and worship Him for all His good deeds. It is altogether different to have Him abide in us.

To permit or allow Him to have His way in us is definitely our highest calling in God. It is here where the idea of an exchanged life starts to take real shape and makes our relationship with Christ take on a fuller meaning.

As the Scripture lays it out: **"Abide in Me, and I in you,."**

This is truly the pattern for anyone who desire to walk close to Christ and yearns deep within, to know Him, as Paul so much longed to do when he said, **"that I may know Him and the power of His resurrection, and the fellowship of His sufferings, being conformed to His death."** (Philippians 3:10)

Stepping into Him is not only a cliché, but a potential reality for those who are willing to pay the price of dying to self, allowing room in their lives to have Jesus grow within. It is not until this reality begins to take shape, that a believer starts to really know and understand the heart and mind of God.

Walk It Out!

My aim today is to ask myself the honest truth, I know that I abide in Him but does He abide in me? Have I given Him total reign in every area of my life?

My Prayer

Dear Jesus — I know that I have made many promises to You. Some I have kept, and some I have broken. I ask you to forgive me for the ones that I have broken. Perhaps, I was looking at my own interests and never considered You, as I was breaking my vow or covenant with You. I do want you to ABIDE in me! Please don't ever walk away from my life God. There is nothing I would rather do, than to abide in You and You in me! Amen.

Day 4

The Spirit of Willingness!

"Let this mind be in you which was also in Christ Jesus, who, being in the form of God, did not consider it robbery to be equal with God, but made Himself of no reputation, taking the form of a bondservant, and coming in the likeness of men. And being found in appearance as a man, He humbled Himself and became obedient to the point of death, even the death of the cross." (Philippians 2:5-8)

Standing in the presence of Jesus this early morning, the Holy Spirit brought to my mind this very subject, the spirit of willingness. What is the spirit of willingness? It is a spirit that is always willing to do what God desires! It is more intrigued with God's plan and purpose than its own plan; it occupies itself with pleasing the Father in every way. Jesus had this.

Because Jesus was willing to make Himself of no reputation . . .

He was willing to become a servant. Jesus didn't think it lowly to be a servant unto others. He didn't see Himself less in comparison to others simply because He served them. This is definitely a lesson for us to grasp.

He was willing to humble Himself. Humility in its basic form means putting the Father's wishes before your own wishes. Jesus left all His heavenly estate for the sake of pleasing the Father. True service is never about us; it is always about others! Making yourself of no reputation or desiring to be somebody in this world must be dealt with. We can't love ourselves and love God; He must have the preeminence in all things.

He was willing to obey to the point of death if He had to. Lastly, Jesus was not only willing to leave His good place in the heavenlies, but also to die for the sake of God's purpose. How many of us are willing to lay down our lives to the point of death for the sake of the gospel?

Walk It Out!

My desire is to evaluate my heart and see if I am still walking in the spirit of willingness. I don't want to allow my flesh or old self to overtake the will of God in my life. Am I still willing to die for the sake of Christ? Or is this fire gone from me? Evaluate.

My Prayer

Heavenly Father, I see the life of Jesus as my example. I want to be like Jesus in all things. I want His passion, desire, and purpose to be my own. Father, taking the life of Christ as my primary example, I want to also take the form of a bondservant and make myself of no reputation, not caring what anyone thinks of me and my zeal for God. Release upon me the spirit of willingness in greater ways in all areas of my life. Amen.

Day 5

The Power of Forgiveness!

"For if you forgive men their trespasses, your heavenly Father will also forgive you. But if you do not forgive men their trespasses, neither will your Father forgive your trespasses." (Matthew 6:14, 15)

When it comes to the subject of forgiveness, many shy away from the actual practice of doing it. Some say that forgiveness should always be done — until they are the ones that need to do it.

In spite of what anyone says about forgiveness, Jesus commands us to do it!

We have to realize that people will always surround us and the chances of them offending us, will always be present. Though we get offended and hurt by others, we are still called to forgive those who do us wrong. This is part of the narrow road Jesus calls us to walk out.

When I think of walking in the power of forgiveness — this is a willful choice that a true disciple of Jesus is willing to make. Some believers feel that they can get away with it (unforgiveness) because of the deep hurt, yet God has others who are not allowed by the Holy Spirit to hold grudges, hurts, or betrayals.

Let me ask you: Has anyone offended you? Are you hurt because of it? If you are carrying unforgiveness, then the calling is to forgive, and to release yourself from the bondage of carrying those chains around you. Unforgiveness puts chains around your life and binds you to the pain.

How can anyone release themselves from the unforgiveness they carry against an individual? We must first, forgive from the heart those who have offended us, and secondly, we must then release them by praying for them.

Walk It Out!

My goal this morning is to make a list (whether visible or mental) of people that I have something against because of past offenses. Be it my acquaintances, friends or enemies — I must forgive them for ALL offenses and then pray for God's blessing upon their lives. Only by doing this can we find true peace and release.

My Prayer

Lord Jesus, my prayer this morning is for You to forgive me for carrying unforgiveness in my heart towards people who have offended me. I ask that you help me overcome this. Also, I don't only want to forgive them, but I also want to bless them. Take me to this higher place in God! Amen.

Day 6

Keep Praying Until . . .

“Then the Lord said, ‘Hear what the unjust judge said. And shall God not avenge His own elect who cry out day and night to Him, though He bears long with them? I tell you that He will avenge them speedily. Nevertheless, when the Son of Man comes, will He really find faith on the earth?’” (Luke 18:6-8))

In meditation today, I heard the Spirit of the Lord tell me to continue persevering in the things that I have set my heart to do. I felt the Lord tell me to press on and not give up because of the way I have been feeling emotionally due to my lengthy fast.

Giving up is so natural for most people, that the temptation to do it is always there. I pray to the Lord that He will give me the strength to finish my race. God knows I need His Spirit to empower me and enable me to soar on eagles’ wings!

When the Lord gives us directives, they serve as motivators. They provide power just like fuel provides for an engine. The Lord gave me several things to go after in this fast, and by His grace, I intend to get them!

As I heard the Lord speak to me today, the story mentioned above hit me. It revealed to me what actually takes place behind the veil. Here's what I gather: The Lord hears my prayer and for whatever heavenly reason, He doesn't answer right away. Actually, He seems to prolong the process of answering. As I continue to come day in and day out in prayer, the Lord begins to take notice of my persistence. It is here where the magic happens!

The Lord will pick up my cause because of my persistence and perseverance! This I do believe. Even so, come Lord Jesus.

Walk It Out!

My desire today is to position myself for the coming answer. I know God has heard my cry, and I know He will answer me! My goal is to keep pressing on until the answer comes, until the breakthrough takes place, until He answers me. I also know that when He answers my prayer— it will come speedily!

My Prayer

Heavenly Father, I need your strength today. I need your vision for my cause to increase. I need heaven to come down upon me and direct my emotions, decisions, and actions. I yearn for a touch of your Spirit. Quicken me oh Lord today, I pray. Amen.

Day 7

Time to Stand Still & Consider!

"Listen to this, O Job; Stand still and consider the wondrous works of God." (Job 37:12)

If there was ever a weakness of weaknesses in us as a people of God, I would have to say it is impatience! The lack of being patient for things to unfold or come to pass, has always been a struggle for people since the world began. It is no different today in our hurry-hurry world!

There are many tedious things that surround us. If we would only take the time to observe with caution, we would learn a great deal.

Some of the most common character builders can be seen as: standing in line at a bank, or waiting in line to pay at the supermarket or sitting at a stoplight for a lengthy amount of time.

Yet more serious matters may include waiting on a doctor's evaluation, or acquiring important documents that could alter your course in life— these are all heavy-duty tests of character.

In all this, God continues to challenge us to be still and consider the works of His hands. God does things that only He can do and make things good for us in spite of how we feel.

He can be trusted with our lives for He looks for our best interest. This He does consistently!

Let us look quickly at two Hebrew words:

1) ***to stand still***—This means to stand firm. We are called to stand firm in who God is.

2) ***to consider***— This means to give careful thought or consideration to something.

The call I feel from the Lord right now, is to stand still and consider all that He is longing to do. Not only what He did yesterday, but what He is doing today and for what He is about to do in the future!

Walk It Out!

I want to learn to walk in this even more. I have perhaps been a bit startled by outward circumstances, and for this I repent of my lack considering what God can do. My heart longs to be a man who stands still and considers the works of God!

My Prayer

Jesus, teach me to walk in the power of being still and considering the wonderful and powerful things you do in my life. Never let me settle for the ideas that the world offers. Don't let me panic when the wheels fall off! Give me eyes to behold your awesomeness in all things! Amen.

Day 8

We Are in His Hands!

"Then the Lord answered Job out of the whirlwind and said..." (Job 38:1)

Is there ever a moment when you feel that all is lost and your life is totally out of control? I have been to this place so many times. I ask the question for the simple reason that this even happens regularly to people of faith.

If you have been walking with Jesus for at least six months, I would venture to say that you have already faced some time of adversity in your life. The Bible says something very interesting about tests and trials. Listen to this: **"These trials will show that your faith is genuine. It is being tested as fire tests and purifies gold—though your faith is far more precious than mere gold. So when your faith remains strong through many trials, it will bring you much praise and glory and honor on the day when Jesus Christ is revealed to the whole world."** (1 Peter 1:7)

It is my opinion, and only my opinion, but I do feel that God allows these situations to arise and awaken our faith and trust in Jesus. Do we truly understand what the Lord's intentions are when our world sends us on a tailspin? Too often our lives are focused on being secure and in cruise control mode, if you will.

However, the Spirit of the Lord has another thing in mind. It is to train us in the area of faith and to see God, even when He is invisible! Do you get me? We will see the fruit of our perseverance.

As we are being challenged in our faith, know that God will not abandon or forsake us; the Lord will speak out of the whirlwind and bring us words of comfort, peace, and joy. He is still King over the floods!

Walk It Out!

My intention today is to trust my King with my whole life. I want to walk blindly with Him and know that in every instance and at every turn, He is watching my every move.

My Prayer

Precious Jesus—open the eyes of my heart and release upon me the ability to see Your mighty hand leading the way! I am in so much need of your presence in my life— please lead me Holy Ghost! Speak my Lord, speak my Lord— for your servant is listening. Amen.

Day 9

The Violent Fire of His Presence!

"But when Paul had gathered a bundle of sticks and laid them on the fire, a viper came out because of the heat." (Acts 28:3)

It is my belief, and I have lived to see this: Nothing exposes our sins and our compromises like the fire of God can. Let me also add this: Nothing exposes our character flaws like God's purifying fire! Have you found this to be true?

Where do we find this kind of fire? Where can this fire be experienced or felt? I must say that this fire can only be found in the very presence of God. When the fire of the Lord is kindled in your heart because you have spent serious time in prayer and in fasting— His fire will burn and consume all the dross in us!

Either the Holy Spirit brings conviction to our wayward self, or He will allow crises to arise in our midst, to test us and consume us in a darkness that has been latent in our carnal nature.

The need for His holy fire has never been greater in our hearts; we need His consuming fire!

It is not enough to have external experiences anymore. Bible reading, worship singing, and opportunities to help those who are less fortunate, will never substitute the manifest presence of God in our life. There has to be more than just going through the motions of being a Christian. Our hearts must be stirred violently by His Spirit!

A note of interest: Where there is no prayer life, (the kind that manifests the presence of His glory) there will be no heavenly consuming fire. If there is no fire, then darkness will set in and pull that servant of God down to the abyss! Selah.

Walk It Out!

My heart's desire is to experience His manifest presence every time I meet with Him. I don't want to live a life of prayer that does not produce His holy fire in me. I want to live with the urgency that God's fire is required daily—not just on special encounters, but on daily ones too!

My Prayer

Holy Spirit, please hear my cry! I don't only want your fire, but I realize more and more how much I need it. Will you visit my cold heart? Will you manifest Your glory to me on a daily basis? Oh! precious Spirit, let your fire come and consume all my darkness and selfishness! Amen.

Day 10

What a Finish!

"Now the Lord blessed the latter days of Job more than his beginning." (Job 42:12)

What a finish Job had! The way Job began this trying journey— one would never even fathom that things would end up in such a blessed state for this man. I don't even think Job had a clue of where all this was heading— his trials, his crazy friends, and his late encounter with God in chapter thirty-eight. Wow.

As I pondered the words written here in Job 42:12, I can only be overtaken by the mercy of God over this man Job. Did Job deserve this? Probably not! Why would God take away everything from this man and then give all of it back multiplied?

I do believe that the Lord blesses us for a season with the intention to use us in blessing others. Once that season has passed, God comes and takes it all away and proceeds to prepare us for the next season of our lives. It doesn't always happen this way, but by the looks of it, it seems that all creation works this way, thus the four seasons of the year.

Here's what I believe happens to God's servants when they become hungry for more of God:

I believe God visits them first, then God evaluates their present spiritual state. After the evaluation is completed, the Lord proceeds to remove everything that they hold dear to so tenaciously. Once all material things have been removed, once all rights have been surrendered to God, the man is purified by the hand of God. Once the man is purified by the Holy Spirit's fire, that man can be trusted again with God's goods. It is here, where God pours out of Himself into this new man and everything that that man receives will be in a refined form!

Walk It Out!

My goal today is to allow the Holy Spirit to evaluate my spiritual state. God knows that I long to please Him in all things. Obviously, my heart has grown fond of many earthly things, yet in my spirit, I long to touch God—within me, there is an unceasing yearning to see Him once again in all His glory!

My Prayer

King Jesus, you know my yearning heart! I can only ask that you would manifest Yourself to me as the Great I Am! I long to know You not only in the years of old, but in the now! Take me to Your secret place, and let me lay there awhile." Amen.

Day 11

An Unquenchable Fire!

"Then Paul dwelt two whole years in his own rented house, and received all who came to him, preaching the kingdom of God and teaching the things which concern the Lord Jesus Christ with all confidence..." (Acts 28:30, 31)

Did Paul have difficult moments? Did Paul suffer greatly for the sake of the gospel of the kingdom? You bet! In spite of all this, the Apostle Paul never even considered quitting or turning his back on Christ.

His message was simple: To preach the kingdom of God and to teach the things which concern the Lord Jesus Christ with all confidence. This was Paul's heart.
What is the message of the kingdom of God?

The message of the kingdom of God is a message that God the Father sent His only begotten Son to the world, and that whosoever believes in Him may have life eternal and will be restored to his original place and purpose in God, through Christ!

Furthermore, Paul also had another burden: To be occupied with things that concern the Lord Jesus Christ. What are those things? What things concern Christ? I believe these things have to do with our allegiance to Jesus, our passion for Jesus, and our obedience to Jesus in spite of adversity (the flesh, the world, and the devil.)

As we offer our hearts in devotion to Christ, let us make sure that our devotion is done with fire, passion and obedience.

Walk It Out!

In meditating on the life of this great apostle, I am continually challenged to press on with a full-hearted zeal after Him. I don't believe that there is an easier way to please the Father, then for one to offer it ALL at the altar of sacrifice!

As the Hymn writer so eloquently put it:
All to Jesus, I surrender,
All to Him I freely give.
I will ever love and trust Him,
In His presence daily live. *- Author Unknown*

My Prayer

My Lord, please hear my humble cry. I don't have what it takes to get to the place my heart yearns for. To live like this great apostle, my passion will always be. Take me there— all of me! Today Jesus, I need you more than ever before. Make my prayer and my fast count for something! Amen.

Day 12

In All Things, Give Thanks!

"...in everything give thanks; for this is the will of God in Christ Jesus for you." (1 Thessalonians 5:18)

This morning I awoke with the desire to give thanks to God. As difficult as things may seem around me, the Lord says for me to give thanks in all things. We must learn to give thanks by faith, but not because we feel good or only when we feel good!

As adverse as life may seem, and as hard a situation may look, always know that it is God who has brought us to this place— it's a place where one is broken by God for the sake of God, which in turn, will bring us to our destiny in God.

Things may not be going great for us, nevertheless, we are commanded to give thanks in everything. Obviously, most people don't give thanks, even when things are going well, much less when things are not looking good! Don't let this be you. Look around you, God is all around you. Give thanks now.

Here's a few things I began to hear the Spirit of the Lord share with me:

Be thankful for being alive! God has given us a life so that we may acknowledge Him for it.

Be thankful for daily bread. God's provision upon you and your family is a testimony to God's faithfulness. He has done great things!

Be thankful for your lot in life. All that you have faced in times past, the things you are facing now, and the things that you will face in the future— are all part of your lot in life. God has made it so!

Walk It Out!

Appreciation for all that God is and what God has done in my life should always take center stage. Giving thanks to the Lord should always be a priority. My goal today is to acknowledge the greatness and faithfulness of God in my life, family and ministry. I must learn that I am where I am, simply because God has intentions of training me here!

My Prayer

Father, forgive me for not acknowledging you on a daily basis. Please quicken my heart to be a man who knows the value of giving thanks in all things. I don't want to miss what you are doing in me and around me. Teach me the art of appreciation! Amen.

Day 13

God's Mending Business!

"He heals the brokenhearted and binds up their wounds (curing their pains and their sorrows)." (Psalm 147:3) Amplified Bible

During my time of fasting and prayer, God has been showing me His heart. He has shown me how He feels about certain matters and has revealed what His real intentions are for me. I do feel that my life is becoming more in tune with His purpose and plan, and how He is aligning my emotions and healing my heart from past hurts and wounds.

Being under the Lord's covering is truly a beautiful thing. Allowing Him to be Your Healer is truly the key to being healed internally. It is my conviction that apart from Him, we wouldn't be able to overcome inward pain. Let me share with you the following . . .

As I spent time in prayer today, the Lord gave me a vision:

In this vision I saw the hand of the Lord sewing two pieces of cloth together. The two pieces of cloth appeared to have been cut in half and were now being put back together. I noticed that the Lord started sewing from the bottom up! Another thing I noticed was that the Lord was not in a hurry to finish this project, but was patiently sewing with perfection. I remember thinking, is He going to finish at that speed? Vision ended.

If you have been through any painful ordeal or are presently facing a tear in your life, let me tell you this: God is going to mend you up! It might take some time to get it done, but He will eventually put you back together again. He will bind up your wounds and heal your broken heart!

Walking It Out!

My desire today is to learn to be patient with all that God is doing in my life— though it might not be easy, it is a must! Trusting God with the process of healing is a very difficult thing to do when you are hurting deep within and find yourself severely emotionally bruised. Most of life's greatest lessons are learned in the fiery furnace of adversity.

My Prayer

Sweet Jesus, please carry me today! I need you more than ever before. I know I can trust You with my whole life. Don't ever let me fall into the hands of my own wicked thoughts; allow me to see Your glory in my struggle. Help me stand! Amen.

Day 14

Experiencing More of Him?

"And those who know Your name will put their trust in You; For You, Lord, have not forsaken those who seek You." (Psalm 9:10)

In much of the preaching and teaching of our day, which in my opinion, is shallow in content and void of spiritual power, people are left empty and destitute in their spirit. The lack of spiritual power and authority coming from the servant of the Lord, has to be one of the most embarrassing expressions and representations of Christ in the church today!

There are lots of fancy words, intellectual thoughts, well put together sentences, impressive illustrations, and as if that was not enough, the theatrics accompanied by a great lighting system, seems to be the focus of preaching ministry today.

I say all that to say this: In spite of all the external factors, the power of Christ is not present. There are people talking about Someone that they don't even know! I'm speaking about Christ the Lord. I mean, they know of Him, but they don't know Him!

Much of the struggle in people today is that they don't know Christ as King and Lord; they might know Him as Savior, but don't know Him as an intimate God who desires to be intimate with us.

In trying to overcome difficult situations and circumstances, or making every effort to stand in the midst of adversity, I don't need to know who Jesus is, I need to know Him, as the Person He is! Do you see this?

Notice the words above in Psalm 9, **"And those who know Your name will put their trust in You."** The word know in Hebrew means, to know experientially.

It's not just about knowing Him but also experiencing Him. If we know Him, He will take care of everything else! I believe this.

Walking It Out!

Today, I have purposed in my heart to know or better, to experience Christ in deeper ways! It is my longing and my heart's desire to become more intimate with my Lord and King. Through the fasting prayer, I can see and experience how this is taking effect even now.

My Prayer

Jesus, today I open my whole being to know You in more intimate ways. I am in so much need of knowing You and pleasing you with my whole life. I have seen You in Your glory in times past; I am calling out for another touch of Your glory in me! Amen.

Day 15

Living Inside God's Sphere & Timing!

"And He has made from one blood every nation of men to dwell on all the face of the earth, and has determined their pre-appointed times and the boundaries of their dwellings..." (Acts 17:26)

In closing fifteen days of my prayer fast today, the Spirit of the Lord brought to my memory the notes I had prepared for my seminar earlier today. I taught about how the Lord has put us all in His timing and His space for us to live powerfully for Him, within His perfect will.

There is a sphere, an environment, and a specific timing God has allotted to His creations where they can learn about Him. Yes, the goal is to learn about Him, to love Him, and to serve Him with single-hearted devotion.

In my pursuit for God, I have come to the realization that anything outside of His sphere and timing, will not work out for me. It will bring pain, confusion, anger, and even outright rebellion into my life.

When the Lord created us, He placed us somewhere— that somewhere has a time and a place. It is this time and place that God uses to do His work in us. The boundaries that He has given us are not to restrain us, but rather to protect us. We must know this.

Too often, we don't like where we have been placed. We tend to complain and whine about our lot in life. For your knowledge, this behavior only hinders God's plan for our lives!

The time and space where God has placed us, is a big part of the process of maturity for us. We cannot afford to discard it; we can't make light of it, lest we end up in the wrong place at the wrong time— and end up worse, as a consequence of our lack of understanding.

Walk It Out!

I have allowed the Spirit of God to teach me the deeper things of the Lord during my time of fasting and prayer— and this is definitely one of the things God has highlighted in my life as a need. I need to learn to live in the sphere God has given me and move in the timing God has allowed me to have. My goal is to be patient with any of the processes God might have in store for me.

My Prayer

Blessed King, please forgive my anxious heart. I know that these are times of growing in revelation; times of entering into the depth of Your Spirit. Please overtake me with Your love, and cause me to run after You, as to always please You! Amen.

Day 16

From the Dust of the Ground!

"Then the Lord God formed man from the dust of the ground and breathed into his nostrils the breath or spirit of life, and man became a living being." (Genesis 2:7 - Amplified Version)

After seeking God and pressing into Him during this fast, I felt that today was the beginning of a new level of intimacy with Him. It has taken me sixteen days of prayer and fasting to get to this place where it all begins to unfold.

As I spent some quality time reading and meditating on the Word of God this morning, the Holy Spirit came and started to teach me about my position in God. The Lord allowed me to see the value of what it means to be formed out of dust, and the grave importance of having Him breathe into me His spirit of life on a daily basis.

Unless we understand what God had in mind when He originally created man out of dust, and unless we see what our position is now, as we come before the Lord in prayer, we might never understand the reason why God's presence visits some and not others!

For starters, we are called to be dependent upon our heavenly Father for everything. The Scripture says that even Jesus Himself prayed, "give us this day our daily bread." Do you see what I am saying?

Our posture should always be that of dust (humility) before God; now, in the presence of man, we should live a life of royalty, for this is our new position in the world. God has made us kings and priests to our God.

Walking It Out!

Today my goal is to enter into the reality of what I really am before the Lord—nothing but dust. This is my key to access God's presence! May my heart always yearn to be in this posture— always mindful that He made me to be a carrier of His breath! Also, to know that without revelation of this kind, it will be impossible to enter into a greater fullness of Christ.

My Prayer

Lord Jesus, thank you for visiting my hungry heart this morning. I look forward to more meetings with you and yearn for your Spirit to show me things that I have yet to learn. I love you my Lord and King! Amen.

Day 17

Recognize the Wiles of the Devil!

"Put on the whole armor of God, that you may be able to stand against the wiles of the devil. For we do not wrestle against flesh and blood, but against principalities, against powers, against the rulers of the darkness of this age, against spiritual hosts of wickedness in the heavenly places." (Ephesians 6:11, 12)

Words, thoughts, ideas, visuals, and many more methods of communication, reach out to us to try and deter us from where God has placed us. Everything in the world is against Christ and His church. One must be aware that the enemy works tirelessly to undo all that God has built.

In my meditation today, I can see how the enemy will allow us to have a victory and enjoy it immensely yesterday, but not today! He will fight with one end in mind— to shut down the fire of God you recently received from the Lord. Have you come to this realization?

Now Ephesians tells us to put on the whole armor of God so that we may stand against the wiles of the devil. What are the wiles of the devil? Wiles are tricks or manipulations designed to deceive someone. Wiles of the devil are those clever schemes used by Satan to ensnare us through temptation, threat, or intimidation.

Stand on Guard!

I have seen this in my life and perhaps you have experienced it in yours: Once we get a victory, we tend to settle, our posture of warfare changes to celebration, and we lay our weapons down. It is here, where the enemy comes in like a flood and sweeps us away! Do you know what I am saying? I hope so.

We can't rest from our battle! If we celebrate with a delicious meal, then hold the spoon or fork in one hand and hold your sword with the other hand! We must always be in war mode!

My fellow soldier in God's army, if you have fallen, then be quick to get up once again. It's not how many times we fall—it's about how quick we get back up! The battle is not over until it's over! I say, "Arise in the name of Jesus!"

Walking it Out!

I have experienced this type of defeat countless times; it is very disheartening! You make every effort to gain victory over temptation and sin, only to see it all slip away by the spirit of slumber! My goal is to arise in His Name today against all wiles of the devil and not buy into the devil's schemes.

My Prayer

Heavenly Father, I come to you today in a spirit of repentance for letting my guard down and allowing the lies of the enemy to lead me away from Your presence. Please forgive my wavering faith! I ask you to cleanse my heart and mind and restore the passion for Jesus one more time. Amen.

Day 18

The Call to Faithfulness!

"Help, Lord, for the godly man ceases!
For the faithful disappear from among the sons of men."
(Psalm 12:1
)

David saw something coming; he saw that the godly servants of the Lord were being challenged. He saw that many who once stood as burning coals for God, had ceased their burning!

If David had been alive today, he would live with a continuously broken heart over this matter. If things were bad back in the days of David, can you imagine today? There has never been such great temptation and such wickedness arrayed against the servants of the Lord, like we are experiencing today.

By way of remembrance, let me just say: The call of God upon you and I, is to remain faithful in spite of all the wickedness that surrounds us. We are called to arise with brightness in the midst of a dark and cold world.

The challenge to walk in purity of mind and heart must take priority in the man of God; anything less than a total commitment to the cross of Christ will not do!

Signs of Decline!

David said, **"the godly man ceases!"**
What this means is that before a man begins to show signs or characteristics of unfaithfulness, his moral compass has already been compromised and consequently, his standards have been lowered.

Once a man has taken God's law out of his heart, the first thing that leaves him is his discernment for what is holy and divine, then his direction to follow King Jesus wherever He goes is lost, and finally, his fiery passion to please God is quieted!

It is true, the faithful disappear due to their lack of holiness and separation from this worldly system. If the world catches our eye, it will seduce us and bring us into a whirlwind of despair. Initially, we might not see it this way, we might fight it and say, not me, but just as Jesus wisely prophesied, "**Wisdom is justified by all her children.**" (Luke 7:35)

Walking It Out!

My goal today is to keep guard on this area of my life— the area of holiness unto the Lord. I must pursue the Lord in this mindset: to know and please the Father in all things! Also, to come to a greater understanding that the Lord Himself has set me apart for Himself and that I might continue to abide in that very place where God has placed me.

My Prayer

Precious Holy Spirit— my prayer this morning is that I would be a godly man who never ceases to burn with intense fire before You! That I might always long to please You by being faithful to all that You ask me to do for You and for the advancement of Your kingdom. Amen.

Day 19

Always Before Me!

"I have set the Lord always before me;
Because He is at my right hand I shall not be moved."
(Psalm 16:8)

In my quiet time with God this morning, I entered into Psalm 16 verse 8. What a powerful revelation of the Lord for me, as David the Psalmist unveiled the secret of his success in God.

In reading the Word of God, one can enter into the heart of God and learn His intentions. With principles outlined as people follow God's divine order and commands, one can discover what makes life fruitful and truly abundant in God.

As a matter of fact, if you and I allow the Holy Spirit to teach us in greater depths the lifestyles of biblical characters, we too shall be walking in greater fullness!

David said, **"I have set the Lord always before me..."** What

David is really saying here is that he has willfully chosen to put God before him, NOT behind him, but in front of him, where David can see God at all times! Wow.

We must learn this to have success in God my dear friends!

The results of doing this are also mentioned here; hear this: Because God is at that particular place or has been placed there by David, (where David can see Him) he will not be moved, shaken, or be found wavering! Do you see now why David was such a successful individual?

In my walk with Jesus, I must always be the follower. He must be first, and I must be right behind Him— this is the divine order. If I allow Christ to be my leader, I shall never lack direction for the rest of my days!

Walking It Out!

Today, I am reminded by the Holy Spirit to evaluate this whole idea of placing Christ before me. I must ensure that He is the One leading my life and I obediently follow with attentiveness and humility. Doing this is a sure guarantee for success in any area. The opposite to this is also true.

My Prayer

Holy Spirit, remind me to always remain a humble servant. Help me to put Jesus first in all things. His opinion and His agenda must always take priority. After I receive instruction from the Lord, I will arrange my life based on His orders, and not arrange my life based on what I want. Amen.

Day 20

Until I'm Satisfied!

**"As for me, I will see Your face in righteousness;
I shall be satisfied when I awake in Your likeness."** (Psalm 17:15)

Have you ever been at the place where you long for something to happen but you're not fully sure if it ever will? Has your heart ever felt such anticipation for something coming but don't know when or what it is? I have felt this way during this protracted fast.

I recently have been experiencing more of a spiritual numbness in my soul. What I mean by this is that my heart and mind feel numb. I'm not sure I am doing a good job of explaining this emotion, but this is the best I can do to express my feelings.

When I set myself to fast for an extended time, I came before the Lord looking for answers and direction for my life, my marriage, and my ministry. In a strange kind of way, these things have been coming together for me, yet my emotional state is pretty numb.

I shared all that to say that my spirit feels very different. My spirit is full of anticipation, almost as if it knows something I don't. It is something that God has purposely kept away from me until a given time. As the writer said in Songs of Solomon, **"I slept but my heart was awake!"**

I am presently experiencing this.

My soul is weary and without emotion, yet my spirit— thirsts and hungers for more of His presence. David said something very deep here: **"I shall be satisfied when I awake in Your likeness."**

This is the very yearning desire I have, that to be satisfied, I must awake in His likeness!

Walking It Out!

My plan is to keep myself occupied in seeking Him in His word, to allow His Spirit to enlighten my eyes, and for my heart to remain pliable before Him. Also, patience must be practiced to a higher degree and humility along with contriteness of heart, must be embraced more fervently.

My Prayer

Heavenly Father, who knows me better than You? I come before You with thanksgiving and appreciation for Your great mercy upon me. I am very thankful for my lot in life and for all the opportunities that You have afforded me to grow and mature in Your love. My simple prayer is that you would teach me to walk in Your patience; also, that I may see the blessing of my journeys and not become discouraged with what my natural eyes see, and my natural eyes hear. I entrust myself into Your care, my precious loving Father. Amen.

Day 21

It's About His Power!

"Some trust in chariots, and some in horses;
But we will remember the name of the Lord our God."
(Psalm 20:7)

In my pursuit of God this early morning, I am brought into the reality of how God makes things happen for His children. All breakthroughs are accomplished by His Holy Spirit!

In our natural way of thinking, we tend to assume that things just happen through human effort. Too often, we become disillusioned by this way of thinking. We set ourselves up for failure when we try to figure God out. Have you ever done this? I mean, are you guilty of ever doing this?

As I meditated, I was reminded by the Lord that His work is done by His Spirit. God's works are not done by our intellect, ability, or talent. God will use our talent and ability, but things are not initiated by our own doing.

As a matter of fact, when things are initiated by us or originate from our own minds, it usually doesn't end well. Unless the Spirit of the Lord is the One who initiates the idea, we will end up in a spiritual shipwreck.

Too often, I have heard believers plead with God about certain matters or adverse situations that they got themselves into; they want God to intervene in something that God never initiated. They launched out into the deep and now are in desperate need of a lifesaver!

You and I are called to move by the power of the Spirit. Here's what I have learned: Whatever it takes for me to move forward in my life, if I am patient and learn to wait for God's prophetic word, a release to press forward will come!

If we are patient, and if we are in tune with God, we will reap an awesome harvest of blessings.

Walking It Out!

I do believe that too often I have grown weary and impatient with the Lord. I have been guilty of jumping the gun too many times, and I am not happy about that! Actually, the consequences have been devastating. As the Scripture above says, "**Some trust in chariots and some in horses...**" This statement has to be the most convictive of all phrases, for my flesh has a tendency to trust in what I can see and feel, and not in the prophetic word of God.

My Prayer

This morning I come to you my Lord and King once again. My prayer is that I may be established in Your prophetic word and not in my own interpretation of life. I want to see things from your perspective; I want to feel Your heart and understand Your intentions for me. Lord help me to walk with you at the highest level possible. In this fast, show me Your face and Your glory one more time! Amen.

Day 22

I Will Wait!

"Indeed, let no one who waits on You be ashamed..." (Psalm 25:3a)

Pressing into this fast, I find myself with very few words to say and very few petitions to make. The fast has been a challenge in so many ways, but even more challenging as I learn to wait upon God for His Spirit to direct me in the way I should go, not to mention the thoughts I need to renew my mind for this season.

The Scripture that I used here came out of my quiet time, as I pondered upon the Lord's plans for my future. The petition here is for God to honor those who wait upon Him. The word wait means to hope in someone to have trust or confidence in someone; especially in regards to the future.

I believe that there are seasons where the Lord keeps us waiting; when I say waiting, I mean waiting. No forward motion to speak of, and no emotion to accompany our acts of obedience, just plain waiting upon God until He reveals and empowers us!

I have learned an important principle as I have fasted these days. I have learned that God is sovereign, and He does what He needs to do, when He feels He needs to do it. My attitude should be that of a servant waiting patiently for God to speak or be directed by His Spirit.

I do believe that I will never be put to shame for waiting upon God. He shall take up my cause and not deny me whatever it is that my heart longs for. I trust Him fully and will not give up until He comes forth in a glorious revelation!

Walking It Out!

As I have been in the quietness of spirit before the Lord, it is my desire to press deeper into His heart. My longing for Him to appear and show me His face has increased. Now, in my emotions, I don't feel them in sync with my mind—therefore, I must press on by faith, until the Lord releases His blessing.

My Prayer

Dear Holy Spirit, I need to see Jesus! My heart longs to have a breakthrough in the Spirit, but I feel that there is a way to go before I touch the hem of His garment! I am in dire need to meet my King face to face. Will you anoint me and help me get there, precious Spirit? Amen.

Day 23

I Love Him but Do I Respect Him?

"Who is the man that fears the Lord?
Him shall He teach in the way He chooses.
He himself shall dwell in prosperity,
And his descendants shall inherit the earth.
The secret of the Lord is with those who fear Him,
And He will show them His covenant." (Psalm 25:12-14)

Too often, I hear believers cry out for more of Christ; for a greater revelation of His Spirit and His word— yet very few of us cry out for a greater revelation of what it means to fear the Lord.

In the Psalm written above, the word fear means to have a profound respect for someone, mainly God. The definition of respect in Webster's Dictionary is : an act of giving particular attention : CONSIDERATION. a: high or special regard : ESTEEM. b: the quality or state of being esteemed. My dear friends, in my seeking after God's heart, I have discovered that true access to a greater revelation of who Christ is, starts with fearing Him and respecting Him; it is here that we will find the secret key that unlocks every door in God. As the Scripture also states, **"The fear of the Lord is the beginning of wisdom."** (Proverbs 9:10)

Once we understand that this is the way to know God in deeper ways, He will proceed to teach us in the way He chooses. He can't teach someone who doesn't respect Him; He can't influence a heart that is set on pleasing itself and not God!

In entering this life, there is nothing but prosperity and blessed promises for those who walk in His ways. Remember: His ways are not our ways! There is a totally different highway for those who choose to fear Him!

In closing these thoughts, the Psalm also states that the secret of the Lord is with those who fear Him and further adds that, "He will show them His covenant."

Everything you and I long to see, hear, and know, yes, the most intimate of details, can all be acquired in the presence of the Lord.

Walking It Out!

This morning's desire is to learn to walk in the fear of the Lord at a higher and more responsible degree. I don't want to miss out on anything God has been storing up for me. I want God to continually trust me with His secrets; for the Lord to unveil His deepest longings on me!

My Prayer

Blessed Savior, I worship You with all my heart today. You are the reason why I have life. You have called me Your own, and I don't want to disappoint You, my Lord and King. Please keep me in the narrow path and don't allow the wicked one to come and touch me. I love You Jesus! Amen.

Day 24

One Thing I Desire!

"One thing I have desired of the Lord,
That will I seek:
That I may dwell in the house of the Lord
All the days of my life,
To behold the beauty of the Lord,
And to inquire in His temple." (Psalm 27:4)

This meditation of David has to be in the heart of every true seeker of Christ. To be in love with God to such a degree, is what true worshipers aspire to find. Count me in!

Seeking God during my extended fast, I have come to this place of desiring God's best for my life, my marriage, my ministry, and anything that He is willing to reveal. It is a genuine heart-cry in my spirit.

While praying and chewing on this portion of Scripture, I have come to understand that David's heart was to **"dwell in**

the house of the Lord all the days of [his] life."

As noble and humble this petition was, this was not David's real reason for wanting to be in the house of the Lord. His real reason comes on the next line: **"To behold the beauty of the Lord, and to inquire in His temple."**

It's obvious to me that David had experienced something very different than most of his friends or contemporaries. David was not a stranger to the beauty of God! David had experienced God in many ways and was now coming back for more! David also knew the secrets of God and wanted to spend his whole life learning from God.

Let me just say that there is no temple in the world so beautiful that it would hold my attention, and especially not to keep me there for the rest of my life. But to have the presence of God visit me— to have the Holy Spirit allow me to behold the beauty of the Lord— I can now see why David desired to be in the temple of the Lord!

Walking It Out!

It is my desire today to make this longing for the beauty of the Lord my real passion. Ministry is great, but ministering to Him and beholding His beauty, is even greater! I desire to grow in this passionate desire, and want to see Him in all His beauty!

My Prayer

My precious Lord and Father, please help me to grow in godly desires. I want to experience more of what David experienced; so help me pursue You like David did! During this season of prayer and fasting, Lord, cause me to see You every single day. Amen.

Day 25

The Art of Twisting!

"Wait on the Lord;
Be of good courage,
And He shall strengthen your heart;
Wait, I say, on the Lord!" (Psalm 27:13)

What a set of verses! The Psalmist David here says to **"wait on the Lord; Be of good courage, and He shall strengthen your heart!"**

Wow. Have you ever heard such consoling words from a human being? This man knew God; this man understood the faithfulness of God; yes, David was convinced that if he just waited upon God, everything would be alright! Have you experienced duress in your own heart? How about discouragement or lack of love or acceptance? David found refuge in waiting upon the Lord.

Now, let us see the word wait in its original Hebrew. The

word wait means the following: (prob. orig. twist, stretch, then of tension of enduring, waiting: Assyrian û ii, i. wait, û, cord; Arabic (qawiya) be strong, (quwwatun) strength, also strand of rope; Syriac (qawi) endure, remain, await,(qwoye) threads, so spider's threads, web).

Many of the Hebrew words are pictorial, so in their definition they always paint a picture.

Here's what I believe David saw. In waiting on the Lord, what it meant to David, was a strand of thread being twisted with another strand. I believe David saw himself as one strand of thread and he also saw God as a strand of thread. Waiting simply meant taking two strands of thread and making them one (by entwining by twisting them. He proceeded to say that if we wait upon the Lord, He will strengthen our hearts!

Here's the revelation— waiting upon God, means that we become one with God. It is here where our strength is found, it's found in our intimacy with Jesus!

Walking It Out!

I'm personally in a season of waiting. It is not as easy as David makes it sound. As a matter of fact, it is perhaps one of the hardest things to do, if you are looking for some quick answers! To wait upon the Lord is a big boys game; waiting upon God is never easy for the flesh, yet it is the only way out of any demise! David understood this, and it is my desire to understand it as well.

My Prayer

Oh, my beautiful King— today I humble myself before Your throne. I need Your help; I need Your strength! Where else can I go to find my heart's desires fulfilled, but here bowing before You! This morning I yield my time, my talents, my ambitions, and everything else I can think of. I lay all my cares at Your feet and come like a beggar seeking a touch from You. Touch me, Oh God! Amen.

Day 26

The Vision of the Rock!

"You must make for me an altar made of earth, and you will sacrifice on it your burnt offerings and your peace offerings, your sheep and your cattle. In every place where I cause my name to be honored I will come to you and I will bless you. If you make me an altar of stone, you must not build it of stones shaped with tools, for if you use your tool on it you have defiled it." (Exodus 20:24, 25)

Early this morning, the Holy Spirit came to me in a dream. Let me share this prophetic dream with you:

In this particular dream, I saw a rock. The rock was kind of long and very solid. Suddenly, the rock parted in half. After this, two hands appeared from nowhere and one piece was being held by the right hand and the other piece was held by the left hand. After this, I heard a voice that said, "Piece them together with glue!"

Then a response came back saying, "If you use glue, you will ruin it; you will not be able to ever connect it again to its original form!" End of dream.

My interpretation as to what I believe the Lord showed me:

The Scripture that I used at the top of this devotion came to my heart: **"If you make me an altar of stone, you must not build it of stones shaped with tools, for if you use your tool on it you have defiled it."**

What the Holy Spirit showed me here was that there are things that God won't allow to be fixed by human ability, with human reasoning, or through human talent. As a matter of fact, God says if you use human tools, you will defile it. Why would God say something like this?

Let me just define the word defile. The word defile in Hebrews means to make unclean. The Lord doesn't want any flesh touching His handiwork! He doesn't want any type of pollution on things that He puts His seal on. Enough said.

Walking It Out!

My heart today longs to please my God in all things. I don't want to do anything that He doesn't approve of. I don't want to be involved in anything that will profane my life or render me powerless!

My Prayer

Jesus, teach me to hear Your voice during this time of fasting and prayer. Bring the breakthrough upon me! I want to walk on a different dimension with a fresh heavenly mindset for Your glory! Amen.

Day 27

Precious Things Have an Expensive Price!

"Weeping may endure for a night,
But joy comes in the morning." (Psalm 28:5)

Have you ever wondered when a season is going to end, and another will begin? Have you ever said to yourself, One-hundred and ten degrees again! I wonder when all this heat will end?

In some parts of the country, the winter season is long and gray, while in other parts of the nation the weather is extremely hot and unbearable. Does it all end because of our complaining? Obviously not! Does our crying make God take it all away? Well, no!

So, what do we do with austere weather? What do we do when we face something we don't like or appreciate? We endure it anyhow! It all works for our own good; it teaches us to be patient and more persevering.

Let me say something about patience. Patience is the fruit of maturity. As we are being tested, our patience is being worked on. As we persevere with intentional poise, we will discover that God has something at the end of the trial! We usually don't see it while we are facing adversity, but don't let that shed fear upon your heart— we will see His glory!

I'm finding out more and more, as I continue my fast, that things of value have a high price to them. Things of precious value are not cheap. Whatever it is that my heart desires is not cheap—thus comes the agony of digging, searching, and waiting.

The Psalmist said, **"Weeping may endure for a night; but joy comes in the morning."**

It is the same for the struggle one has when seeking God's best! It is painful but rewarding! Only those who pay the price get to take the gold home!

Walking It Out!

I have set my heart today to continue persevering at the well. My goal is to stay put in mind, soul and spirit, until the answer comes. I want to know God in the deepest of ways and walk in His stead, with great intensity!

My Prayer

My humble prayer today, Jesus, is to attain greater knowledge and wisdom of You. I want to understand the things that move Your heart. I want to follow You with a passionate heart and always with great awareness of how intimate I am with You or not! Amen.

Day 28

In the Likeness of His Resurrection!

"For if we have been united together in the likeness of His death, certainly we also shall be in the likeness of His resurrection, knowing this, that our old man was crucified with Him, that the body of sin might be done away with, that we should no longer be slaves of sin." (Romans 6:5, 6)

If there is one thing I'm beginning to understand more and more during my time of fasting and prayer, it is this, the resurrection power of Jesus!

My heart is full of desire to become that for which Christ died. To honor Jesus the King by telling Him that His death was not in vain, and that all He did for me will bear fruit, has to be the greatest honor!

I know that in our institutions today— our churches and people are still made to believe that Christ died at Calvary so that they could be blessed and never have to suffer ever again, yet somehow this message leads people astray. It teaches people to be takers and not givers, to receive healing and not to heal others, to be full of themselves and to not deny themselves.

When I ponder the words found in Romans 6:5, in the likeness of His resurrection, many things cross my mind and heart. It challenges me in a direct way to think like Jesus did, to speak like Jesus did, and to act like Jesus acted while on earth. Resurrection life is the life of Christ displayed with confidence, power, and authority! Anything less than this would not be Christ!

Many have made Christianity a set of rules, behaviors, and rituals. Resurrection power doesn't have a manual, apart from the life of Christ displayed. What are we missing then? We are missing the resurrection power of Jesus in us!

When we die to self, we will be resurrected in power; not until we die though, will the power come!

Walking It Out!

I have been craving for God to use me. God has been craving for me to die! Death comes before resurrection! "If the seed doesn't fall to the ground and die, it abides alone. If it dies, then it will bear much fruit," said Jesus.

My Prayer

Walk with me King Jesus and take me to this place of greater fruitfulness! I want to live all my life for You. Please help me to understand Your heart in deeper ways and move in great ascendancy! Amen.

Day 29

Overcoming Disappointments!

"Why are you cast down, O my inner self? And why should you moan over me and be disquieted within me? Hope in God and wait expectantly for Him, for I shall yet praise Him, who is the help of my countenance, and my God." (Psalm 42:11 - Amplified)

Have you ever failed people? By people I mean friends, family, and those who are close to you? I'm talking about those who look up to you, who trust you, who will do anything to see you succeed? Well, I have.

There is nothing more humbling and difficult to overcome than when other people have been hurt or betrayed by you. It is no easy thing to overcome! The sense of failure is so overwhelming that many have gone into isolation and despair.

Last night the Lord gave me a very powerful dream. I had

a dream that I was working on something at my office, and one of my staff members came in. As I reached out to greet them, they pushed back. I saw their face, and I could see that they were holding great disappointment for something I had committed against them. End of dream.

In retrospect, regarding any event when failing people, I have learned that humility and sincere apologies are God's methods to overcoming the disgrace that one feels for failing others. It is super easy to get down on yourself and beat yourself up for doing so! Do you know what I mean?

In Psalm 42:11, I discovered the Psalmist writing about feeling cast down in his inner self. The emotion of being disquieted within is very painful, and it can end up being very paralyzing to anyone. Yet, in all his downcast emotion, the Psalmist rises above the tempest and the storm and says, **"Hope in God and wait expectantly for Him, for I shall yet praise Him, who is the help of my countenance, and my God."**

The key to overcoming the sense of failure is to put your hope in God and to wait expectantly for Him. Continue to praise Him— only He is able to pull you out of the mire, for He is God!

Walking It Out!

I must keep a posture of praise and worship ever before Him, lest I be taken down by self-pity, guilt and shame. I must allow the Holy Spirit to be my Guide through any disappointing event in my life. He is the help of my countenance!

My Prayer

Precious Holy Spirit, this morning I yield myself to You. Heal my broken heart! I worship You oh Lord, the Lover of my soul. Take me through the tempest and the storms that I face daily. I know You will make me stand in any situation. Amen.

Day 30

The Excellency of the Knowledge of Christ!

"Deep calls to deep in the roar of Your waterfalls; all Your breakers and Your billows have swept over me." (Psalm 42:7) [Holman Christian Standard Bible]

In my time of knowing Jesus my Lord, I have come to the understanding that He is more real than real!

I have set my heart like a flint to go after Him and to grow in the knowledge of Him. This is not a religion I am speaking of, it's the knowledge of knowing this awesome Person called Jesus Christ!

I have a sign in my office that reads, In the morning— give me Jesus! This is what I want my legacy to be. I want to be known as a man of God, who lived and died for Jesus! I have no other deeper passion in my life, other than to grow and know my God in deeper ways.

In my pursuit of God, I have found many others who seek the same thing. They have made themselves available to touch God and to see His glory. This is a great thing.

The sad thing is this: those hungry, passionate seekers of the deeper things of the Lord, are not as many as you would imagine. They are the faithful few that make up the generation of Jacob here on earth. These are the vessels of God who have not put themselves before the Lord. Yes, these are those who have laid it all down as Paul so wonderfully states in Philippians when he says, **"But what things were gain to me, these I have counted loss for Christ. Yet indeed I also count all things loss for the excellence of the knowledge of Christ Jesus my Lord, for whom I have suffered the loss of all things, and count them as rubbish, that I may gain Christ and be found in Him..."** (Philippians 3:7-9)

Walking It Out!

Anything that helps me to know God is what I want to practice. There is only one eternal pursuit worth following and that is to know Christ in deeper ways! I want more of Jesus and by God's grace I shall have more of Jesus!

My Prayer

King Jesus—it is my simple prayer this morning to get to the place of revelation, knowledge, and deeper desires in the move of God for my life. I don't want to miss a thing in God! Holy Spirit, please lead me today with a passionate heart. Amen.

Day 31

Overcoming the Spirit of Lawlessness!

"Therefore, the law is holy, and the commandment holy and just and good." (Romans 7:12)

Have you ever been told to do a certain thing by someone you love and respect, but deep inside you didn't want to? Does it upset you when someone challenges you in any way, shape, or form? Here are some examples: One day that person could call you out and say, You are gaining so much weight; if I were you, I would start working out.

These words, for some reason, end up getting you so upset, that you might express it, or you might hold it in— but the emotion you get is anger and rebellion towards those words (or law).

Suddenly you find yourself fighting something that you did not expect to find within you—it's called the spirit of lawlessness!

This spirit of lawlessness dwells within every human being and its characteristics are all too common. Let me explain further: When driving through a school zone, the lights are blinking, and the speed limit is 15 mph. You see the lights, you see the sign, but something deep within you says, It's ok, go a little faster. You begin to reason why you should go a little faster, or why you are not under any law but the law of God! Then you proceed to speed, when suddenly the police officer pulls you over for speeding in a school zone! (Ouch! Let me just say that the fine will teach you a great lesson.)

The rage deep within you when the police officer is perhaps not scolding you, but maybe challenging your judgment, is inevitable, until you humble yourself before God and realize that the spirit of lawlessness got the best out of you and repent!

Paul says that **"the law is just and good."**

The law of God by its very nature, condemns. It points the finger and calls us out, if we are breaking it. This is what the law is supposed to do— bring conviction for any wrong-doing.

Now, the good thing about the law of God, is that it brings us to Christ. We have a chance to repent after the law of God has convicted us of sin. Once the blood of Jesus is applied, and our hearts restored back to the Father, His joy will flood our hearts once again. This is what walking with Jesus is all about!

Though the law of God brings judgment— His blood is more than enough to cover my guilty stains. **"Mercy triumphs over judgment."** (James 2:13b). Thank You Jesus!

Walking It Out!

I must be better at being on guard through the Spirit of the Lord, to fight against the spirit of lawlessness in my own life. I have seen this horrible spirit bring me down countless times. It is my desire to overcome it by the power of God.

My Prayer

Holy Spirit, this morning I yield myself to Your leadership. I long to have victory over my flesh every day. I ask that You release a greater level of discernment, that I may gain continuous victory over the spirit of lawlessness. In You alone I put my precious trust, Spirit of the living God! Amen.

Day 32

The Meek!

"But the meek shall inherit the earth,
And shall delight themselves in the abundance of peace."
(Psalm 37:11)

Here is a secret with God: The meek (a person characterized by humility) will inherit the earth. The Scripture clearly states a principle on how to gain possession of property by a certain way of being. Through humility, one becomes heir of property that is held by someone else in power!

Is it really humility that gets us there? Well of course not! The Lord gets us to His desired end through our attitude of putting Him first in our lives and in every decision we make. Meek people are people who have been broken by the Lord, just as a horse is broken by its rider before the horse enters training.

Once the Lord finds a meek person, He will shape them into

the vessel He needs. Once shaped and trained, God will proceed to use them for His good pleasure, mainly to expand His kingdom here on earth, by using their gifts and talents.

Now, a meek individual doesn't allow themselves to be led by worldly order, emotion, status, riches, ambitions, and agendas. He follows the Lord's heart for He is possessed by it!

Once the person understands fully that every good and perfect gift comes from the Father of Lights, he can rest with full assurance that God has his life in the palm of His hands. He no longer fears, doubts, or gets anxious about life's woes and circumstances.

Humility makes us meek; if we become meek, God will dwell richly in us; if God is dwelling, then peace will flow like a river! It is the peace of God that we always want!

Walking It Out!

As I meditate upon the Lord's goodness today, I am reminded that although things around me may not be in their proper place or to my liking, God is still the King of the Universe. He is still the Lord of my heart and my whole being. He is still worthy of all my praise! My desire is to be a meek vessel for Him!

My Prayer

Lord, today I call upon you for strength in my inner man. I have a longing to know You, but I have very little fervor today. I need You to visit me once again and vivify my mortal flesh. Come Holy Spirit, I pray. Amen.

Day 33

What an Amazing Love!

**"The steps of a good man are ordered by the Lord,
And He delights in his way.
Though he fall, he shall not be utterly cast down;
For the Lord upholds him with His hand."** (Psalm 37:23-24)

Walking with Jesus has to be the most awesome experience given to the human being. I say this because of the sense of God's leadership in my life. There is an amazing feeling deep within me that says, "God is walking with You no matter where you find yourself, David!"

Sometimes in my walk with God, I get the sense that I am left to deal with life alone. But the fact is that I am never alone! Actually, the Lord continues day in and day out to order my days. God has awesome plans for all who follow His leadership.

What does, "the steps of a good man are ordered by the Lord" mean? Order means to be set up, or established. In other words, the Lord has already ordered my life, and He leads me by His Spirit in the way that I should go.

Does it mean that His way is perfect for me, as outlined by Him? Yes! His way is already designed for my personal success and joy. Now, if I choose to allow myself to pursue another way, if I detour from God's intentional highway for me, I will end up falling (being pulled down by gravity) into a pit.

The interesting thing about my relationship with God is this—He will not allow me to be utterly cast down! He will not allow me to keep falling into my own delusion for long. The Scripture says that He will uphold me with His hand. Now, that is mercy in action!

In spite of my rebellious tendencies, my wayward attitude, and stubborn outbursts— the Lord continues to guide me along the way of righteousness for His good pleasure.

Thank You King Jesus for being always before Me, even when I don't recognize You in the middle of my mess!

Walking It Out!

What a humbling thing this is. To know that God is there no matter what I do or where I decide to go. His mercy is unchanging and renewed daily. For this I am more than grateful to my God! My desire today is to acknowledge His faithfulness and His loving passion for me!

My Prayer

Once again dear Father, I am humbled at the sight of Your loving arms surrounding me. Do I deserve this amazing love? I know I don't! Yet, I cannot run away from Your embrace. You are so good to me, even when I don't deserve such love. Receive my adoration this morning Jesus. I love You. Amen.

Day 34

Lord, Open My Eyes!

"Open my eyes, that I may see..." (Psalm 119:18a)

While in evening prayer today, the Holy Spirit impressed on me some deep thoughts on vision. He spoke to me the value of having vision not only for the natural, but the spiritual as well.

As a matter of fact, everything God has created is set into motion by His spoken word. His spoken word has a powerful creative effect, and from everything that the Lord prophesies or speaks forth, things materialize!

In my pursuit after His heart, the Lord unfolded some interesting things that I want to share with you along the lines of vision or the blessing of seeing what God is saying or doing.

First, I want you to see this Scripture: **"Where there is no vision, the people perish..."** (Proverbs 29:18a)

The word vision means a religious or mystical experience of a supernatural appearance, (that imparts a message) usually through a dream.

If there is one thing that is true here, is that without a vision from heaven, we are limited here on earth. If we don't experience supernatural moving(s) of God in our life through prophetic revelation, we will be limited in our thinking, speaking and in how we take action!

Now, the Scripture clearly states that without vision, "**people perish.**" How is that? What that means is that without a fresh revelation from the Lord, the people won't know what to do, or what to say, or how to act. They will be turned loose and left to deal with life on their own without God's leadership!

As I have pondered these words in my heart, I realize that much of what surrounds me on a daily basis is directed by spiritual forces. Either I am being empowered by the Lord through His Holy Spirit and His very words; or I am being set up for failure by spiritual for-ces of wickedness in high places— all with an agenda to destroy my destiny in God!

Walking It Out!

My desire this evening is to know the mind and will of the Lord for my life. Also, not to allow external situations to govern my internal world. On the contrary, live from the inside out. Allow God to rule and reign in my life and live my life from that perspective on a daily basis.

My Prayer

Precious Spirit of God, please open my eyes, that I may see all that You have destined for me. Help me to see Your hand at work in my life; help me to see the arrangements of love that you have made with me. I don't want to miss out on anything you have already aligned for my life!" Amen.

Day 35

Led by the Spirit!

"For as many as are led by the Spirit of God, these are sons of God." (Romans 8:14)

There is only one true way to live for God— it is by being led by His Spirit! Anything less than the leadership of the Holy Spirit is flesh and will eventually end up in corruption.

The Scripture is clear about who are the children of God— it's those who are led by the Spirit of God. To be led means to willingly undergo an action or course (due to influence). True children of God allow themselves to be influenced by God's Spirit.

I have been on this journey for some weeks now, praying and fasting, for the purpose of aligning my life with the will of my heavenly Father, for deeper intimacy with Jesus and greater communion with the Holy Spirit.

I need more of the Spirit's leadership in my life; actually, I need Him more than I need my next breath! With all this said, I have ventured to seek His heart with full hearted passion and desire.

In the last few days, the Holy Spirit has been talking to me about my position in God. He wants me to gain an understanding of what it means for Him to be first in my life. Along with this, He has spoken to me about divine order and how things need to be done!

There are things that I don't understand about God's way of doing things in certain ways, but I trust His leadership. I will not complain about or criticize my God's leadership! In all this, I must allow Him to be the government in my life. I don't want to take the lead, for I don't know the wilderness like Jesus does.

Walking It Out!

I have determined to make many changes to my life, so that I may accommodate His will for my life. The fasting lifestyle must become part of my whole being. I must allow the Holy Spirit room to work in me and through me! This shift must take root immediately.

My Prayer

Holy Spirit, you have been my Guide from the beginning of my journey with Jesus! You have led me through thick and thin; You have carried me time and time again, on eagles' wings! If it wasn't for You, Spirit of the Living God, I would have despaired and given up. Thank You Father, for the promised Holy Spirit! Lead me Lord, I will follow. Amen.

Day 36

Don't Get Tired!

"So let's not get tired of doing what is good. At just the right time we will reap a harvest of blessing if we don't give up." (Galatians 6:9 New Living Translation)

I want to take this time to express my gratitude to the Lord! I want to acknowledge His keeping power and how He has kept me in the fight for the last few weeks during my protracted fast.

I want to also say that it has been a true challenge, for my flesh in every way possible.

The mind games are beyond anyone can imagine— the lust for worldly delicacies and all it has to offer, are ever so present. Nevertheless, God has been faithful. Though I fall, I know that He is able to make me stand!

While contemplating the onslaught of temptations and all

kinds of ungodly desires, the Holy Spirit brought this word to mind: **"Now to Him who is able to keep you from stumbling, and to make you stand in the presence of His glory blameless with great joy..."** (Jude 1:24).

A very interesting point here is that God is able to keep us from stumbling, and He is also able to make us stand in the presence of His glory, blameless!

The enemy would love to laugh and ridicule the man of God who postures himself for a greater blessing in his life— but the Lord will be his strength and refuge and will exalt him to a place of greater abundance.

Faith in who He is and what He can do has been brought to the forefront time and time again— the ability to walk in full victory has been magnified and the devil knows it!

The word of the Lord for today is, "Don't get tired of doing what is good! There is a time for a great breakthrough just ahead. Just don't give up!"

Walk It Out!

It is not an easy thing to fast for many days, much less to

overcome many temptations while you are experiencing hunger. No wonder Jesus had one of His biggest battles in the wilderness against Satan in Matthew 4. Yet, in all of this, Jesus committed Himself to the Father and His Word. This I must do daily to get the victory!

My Prayer

Jesus, I come to You today with a heavy heart. I ask that You carry me once again. Cleanse my mind, my heart and my hands from sin. Purify me in Your fire and help me to be an overcomer full of Your glory and strength. If I ever needed You Lord, it is now! Amen.

Day 37

The Overcomer!

"For I consider that the sufferings of this present time are not worthy to be compared with the glory which shall be revealed in us." (Romans 8:18)

Overcomers are a breed of servants of God who see the end from the beginning. These servants don't see all the issues that go on in daily life as something to spend much time on; they see tests and adversities as opportunities to grow and develop.

They have been touched by God and begin with the end in mind, God's end!

As I have made it my goal to be an overcomer in my own life, I have discovered that the attitude of an overcomer is very different from the traditional orthodox Christian believer—that one, who measures every little thing that happens to them.

As I have been spending time in His presence these last few weeks with a more intentional approach and allowing the Holy Spirit to align my life, marriage and ministry, I have come to learn that letting God's Spirit be the leader in my life, is the best thing by far!

I do believe that one of the main struggles with believers as they make their effort to walk in God's will, is that they easily get confused by difficulty. It doesn't take much for some brother or sister to fly off the handle!

These servants of God have not seen into the future; they have not tasted of the age to come! No wonder their lives are shallow and lack patience.

One thing I have learned in this season: I can make every attempt to become a better man, yet in my flesh, I will have to fight over and over again. When I fall, I must quickly respond by getting back up! I shall not allow any form of adversity to dominate my thinking! The battle is not over till it is over!

Walk It Out!

My resolve to follow Jesus remains steadfast! I will remember the words of David when he wrote: "Though I walk through the valley of the shadow of death, I shall fear no evil, for thou art with me!" I will make this my song in the night season; I will rejoice in the day season. To God be the glory now and always.

My Prayer

King Jesus, sustain me in every season of my life. I will always sing of the goodness of God over my life. You have been my strong Tower! You have been my Rock! Thank You, Jesus! Amen.

Day 38

God Is for Me!

"What then shall we say to these things? If God is for us, who can be against us?" (Romans 8:31)

From the beginning of creation, God has been after us! He longs to find us, fill us with His Spirit and restore us to His original plan. It has been God's passion to seek us out! Check this out: In pursuit to get us to sit with Him where He is, God even sent His only begotten Son, Jesus— that we may be established in Him. What an awesome loving Father, He is!

I know that many have thought that God's agenda is to destroy or annihilate wicked sinful people. I have even prayed for God to do that to my enemies— to people who have hurt me deeply. Yet, in some strange way, God loves His creation, and has an awesome plan for His children. The only thing missing from the dinner table are those who will listen to Him! Some have by willful choice, made a decision to stay away!

What God will do with wicked people, and how He judges them is really not based on my emotion towards them. God's patience doesn't run out just because mine has! God is altogether different. He thinks differently and moves by a different economy; we are human and see a very limited world ahead of us. We only see a partial view.

Based on all that, I want to say that no matter what God decides to do with the wicked, I know His heart is for me— He is for me! He is crazy about me and wants the best for me! This much I know.

So, if God is for me, who can be against me? It doesn't really matter who arrays against me. I win, because of Jesus!

Walk It Out!

I have set my heart today to rest in His love for me— to know that He is for me and that nothing can hurt me without His knowing. I will bless the Lord at all times, and His praise shall continually be in my mouth.

My Prayer

In just reading the book of Romans my dear Lord, I am challenged one more time by the life of the great servant Paul. The way He knew You; the way He followed You, and the way He endured for You— I want to be that man! Amen.

Day 39

Never Neglect the Spiritual Man!

"Oh, send out Your light and Your truth!
Let them lead me;
Let them bring me to Your holy hill
And to Your tabernacle.
Then I will go to the altar of God,
To God my exceeding joy;
And on the harp I will praise You,
O God, my God." (Psalm 43:3, 4)

For the Lord to send His light and truth into our lives, there has to be a time of cultivation or better stated, a time of intimacy. I see how positioning my heart before Him, brings me to a dimension in the spirit where I can know His thoughts, ideas, and point of view.

Too often, we as human beings tend to leave home without touching the Father's heart; we are quick to get on with our lives without ever acknowledging His glory in the midst of us. Remember: The Lord is all around us—we just don't take time to look for Him!

As I pondered the beauty of the Lord this early morning, I read this awesome contemplation by the Psalmist where he states a very powerful principle for living an effective and efficient life!

Here's what I have learned: Whether I care to admit it or not, I have been guilty one too many times of neglecting the spiritual man. If there is neglect to the spiritual man— know that there are no substitutes for this. One cannot read the Bible, or even do a long fast, to replace this intimacy with God.

You see, to open my heart to King Jesus on a daily basis through personal prayer, this is the key that unlocks my destiny. I will never know what I don't know, if I neglect my personal prayer time with God. I must attend to this fire!

It is my responsibility to get a hold of God and wait patiently for Him to speak to my heart. It is here where instruction, knowledge, and wisdom are exchanged. You see, I'm convinced that all my daily success will flow out of this daily experience!

Just meditate upon how wonderfully and beautifully the Psalmist puts it:

"Oh, send out Your light and Your truth!
Let them lead me;
Let them bring me to Your holy hill
And to Your tabernacle.
Then I will go to the altar of God,
To God my exceeding joy;
And on the harp, I will praise You,
O God, my God."

My harp will only play as an expression and response to what God is doing deep within me. I must minister to the Lord before I minister to anyone else or attend to anything else in my life. This is divine order!

Walk It Out!

Whatever it takes, I must be about my Father's business. This means that I should become more attentive to the tending of the fire at the altar! The fire must never go out!

My Prayer

By Your grace oh Lord, I will be a man of fire! Let me burn until there is nothing left of me. May my living and dying be all about You. Let people see You in me, King Jesus. Amen.

Day 40

Learning to Lean!

"Trust in the Lord with all your heart,
And lean not on your own understanding.
In all your ways acknowledge Him,
And He shall direct your paths." (Proverbs 3:5, 6)

As I come to the close of another season of prayer and fasting in my life, I look around me and my heart is full of joy. My body is weak, but my spirit is filled with the expectation of all that God is going to do due to this fast.

During my time of seeking God, I have experienced much growth in my spirit man; I have seen God do things that have reestablished my faith. I have also experienced great opposition to the movement of God in my life.

I look at the list of things that I had originally proposed to carry out during my fast, and in all the categories, I have seen an increase— a good increase. Fresh direction for my life has blown in like an awesome cold-front on a Fall morning. I thank Jesus for that.

As far as opposition is concerned, I have also seen much of that. The challenging words from the enemy that have come roaring-in saying, "This fast was all for nothing! You will never regain composure on anything! You wasted your time, and you only starved yourself to no avail! Just look around you, what has changed? What difference did that protracted fast make?"

These thoughts and many more have bombarded me in these last few days, and to be honest, it can be discouraging!

When I look around me and ponder the reality of what my eyes literally see, I get to thinking and then saying, Maybe the enemy was right! What difference has this fast made? What on God's green earth was I thinking to set myself up for such a crazy fast as this one?"

No sooner had I said this, suddenly the Spirit of the Lord came and raised up a standard against what was warring in my mind; He spoke to me these comforting words from Proverbs 3:5, 6:

"Things are not what they seem! What you are literally seeing with your natural eyes, is not the reality of what is actually happening in the spirit. Don't trust your own mind and heart and don't lean on your own understanding. David, only acknowledge Me, I am in your midst, I will direct your paths!"

I'm telling you— God is faithful! He will lift me up and bring me into an abundant place.

Walk It Out!

My goal is to press into the spiritual realm and get to know the Lord in deeper ways. I'm like that deer from Psalm 42: **"As the deer pants for the water brooks, so pants my soul for You, O God. My soul thirsts for God, for the living God."** (Psalm 42:1, 2)

My Prayer

Jesus, my Lord and King! I want to thank you for your kind mercy and for showing me that there is so much more in You! You are like an ocean that has no end to its depth; I love You with all my heart. I ask that You visit me in the days to come and show me Your heart and what it is that You are thinking.

As I postiioned my life before You, may Your glory shine forth in me and through me. It is my desire that You be the light of my countenance Jesus! With all the strength that a human being can release, I say, I love You my Lord and King! Amen.

Ministry Resources

Most Shabar Publications products are available at special quantity discounts for bulk purchase for sales promotions, fund-raising and educational needs. For details, write Shabar Publications at mayorga1126@gmail.com.

For the purchase of more books
written by David Mayorga,
***visit our bookstore at*:**

www.shabarpublications. com

Ministry Information

Shabar Publications is a ministry expression under Masterbuilder Ministries, Inc. in Palmhurst, Texas. This publication ministry, was founded and created for the purpose of writing books and distributing them to the body of Christ both locally and globally. The intent behind the idea of publishing these works, is to train and equip the reader to be a more intimate lover of Jesus Christ, our Lord! Out of an intimate life with God, by the grace of God, effective ministry will be the outflow.

For more information regarding this ministry, feel free to email us at: mayorga1126@gmail.com.

www.ingramcontent.com/pod-product-compliance
Lightning Source LLC
Chambersburg PA
CBHW060555100726
47907CB00005B/1370

9781733317498